CARIBBEAN VEGAN

The Way Of The Islands

JAVON S. WOOD & TONY D. FLASH

Flash Supplements LLC

CARIBBEAN VEGAN

First Printing 2021 Written by Javon S. Wood and Tony D. Flash
Cover Design by Erin Babb
Editing, Text Layout, & Formatting by Cheyanne K. Gonzalez
Photos by Freepik
Category: Cookbooks, Food Books, Food and Wine
Library of Congress Control Number: 2021925234
Printed in the United States of America by:
IngramSpark | www.IngramSpark.com

CONTENTS

ACKNOWLEDGMENTS

First, I would like to thank my older brother Tony D. Flash for helping me to remember my worth in the world as a black young man. Also, for motivating me to change my life around to become a better person. Without him in my life I wouldn't be complete. My brother Tony D. Flash is an adroit and talented Black King. He has two of his own books, Nine and Breaking Toxic: Love Yourself First, It's Okay.

Also, I would like to thank my parents, Samuel H. Wood and Catherine A. Simms for being here for me. Without the both of you I wouldn't be here today. I want to thank my father for pushing me to be something in life and keeping me strong throughout my life. You have always inspired me to become better. Also, I would like to thank my beautiful mother for making me happy. She is the World to me. She does everything for me.

Life is an abstract. These three people motivate me and make me stronger in each and in every way. Their love and compassion for me is unimaginable. Making this book with my brother Tony D. Flash inspires me to make more books with him in the future. Thank you for all you have done for me.

Sincerely,

Javon S. Wood

INTRODUCTION

Welcome to the vegan revolution!

We would like to thank you for purchasing Caribbean Vegan, The Way of the Islands. All the support and love that we received while making this fantastic book is greatly appreciated as we did the "impossible". We took some of the most well-known and favorable dishes from each nation in the Caribbean, while also adding some recipes we could not go without. Veganism has now changed the world and it can't be ignored. Eating healthy is a conscious choice, we really are sparing the animals of this land by choosing to go plant based. In this book you'll find recipes that imitate the foods we truly enjoy eating in the Caribbean, and we hope you'll have fun and enjoy them too.

The listed ingredients throughout this book are not all un-common. Believe it or not, when becoming a vegan, you realize the foods you now consume daily have been around you in all the different supermarkets that you may already shop at. Vegan foods have especially started to trend and become more popular within the recent years. Some great places to find the foods listed in the upcoming recipes are your local supermarkets, health food stores, and one of my favorites, the Asian supermarkets. You should be able to locate most if not all of what you need to cook up some delicious Caribbean meals right in the comfort of your home. If for any reason, based on your location or store you can't find any of the ingredients listed, try using alternatives that may be available or order them from online. Within the recipes you'll notice ingredients such as "Vegan Chicken" listed. On the next page, I provided a list of suggested branded products for these vegan ingredients that you may not be too familiar with depending on you level of Vegan expertise, and that will taste great.

INGREDIENT	SUGGESTED PRODUCT	INGREDIENT	SUGGESTED PRODUCT	INGREDIENT	SUGGESTED PRODUCT
Almond Milk	Silk, Almond Milk Original OR Vanilla	Soy Milk	Silk, Unsweetened Soy Milk	Vegan Frog Legs	Dui Ech Chay, Vegan Frog Legs
Chicken Style Seitan	Nature's Soy, Vegan Chicken Seitan	Spelt Flour	Arrowhead, Organic Spelt Flour	Vegan Whipped Cream	Reddi Wip, Non-Dairy Almond Milk Whipped Cream
Coconut Milk	Goya, Coconut Milk	Textured Vegetable Protein	Red Mill, Textured Vegetable Protein	Vegan butter	I Can't Believe It's Not Butter, It's Vegan
Dairy-Free Yogurt	Silk, Almond Milk Dairy Free Yogurt	Tofu	House Food, Organic Tofu, Extra Firm	Vegan Chick'n	Just Like Chicken Textured Vegetable Protein
Vegan Crab Meat	May Wah, Vegan Imitation Crab Steaks	Vegan Beef	Beyond Meat, Beyond Beef Plant Based Ground	Vegan Chorizo Sausages	Field Roast, Spicy Mexican Chipotle Sausages
Young Jackfruit	Native Forest, Organic Young Jackfruit	Vegan Boullion, Chicken OR Beef	Better Than Bouillon, No Chicken Base OR No Beef Base	Vegan Egg	Just Egg, Plant Based Liquid Eggs

Seitan	Uptons Naturals, Seitan, Original	**Vegan Vanilla Frozen Yogurt**	So Delicious, Dairy Free Creamy Vanilla Soy Milk	**Vegan Vanilla Ice Cream**	So Delicious, Dairy Free Oatmilk Creamy Vanilla Bean
Vegan Mayonnaise	Follow Your Heart, Original Vegenaise	**Vegan pork**	Be Leaf, Plant Based Pork	**Vegan Grated Cheddar Cheese**	Daiya, Medium Cheddar Style Block
Vegan Tuna	Vegan Zeaster, Notuna Sashimi OR Good Catch, Fish Free Tuna	**Vegan sausage**	Beyond Meat, Original Vegan Sausage	**Beef Crumbles**	Beyond Meat, Beyond Beef Crumbles
Vegan Mozzarella Cheese	Follow Your Heart, Mozzarella Style	**Vegan Salami**	Yves, Veggie Salami OR Helenic Farms Fig Salami		

Traditional Drinks & Smoothie

Frozen Pineapple Mango Vodka (ALCOHOLIC)

INGREDIENTS
- 1 1/4 cup chopped Pineapple
- 1 cup chopped Mango
- 1 cup Ice
- 3-4 ounces Vodka

Syrup
- 3/4 cup Sugar
- 3/4 cup Water

INSTRUCTIONS
Syrup

1. Put water and sugar into a small pot.
2. Cook on medium until it comes to a boil.
3. Lower heat to a simmer and cook for 10 mins.
4. Set aside to cool.

Frozen Blend

1. In a blender add mango, pineapple, and syrup. Blend until smooth.
2. Add vodka. Blend for a few seconds until combined.

Banana Rum Smoothie (ALCOHOLIC)

INGREDIENTS

- ¼ cup Almond Milk
- 2 tablespoons light Rum
- 2 tablespoons white Creme de Cacao (chocolate liqueur)
- 2 tablespoons Creme de Banane (banana liqueur)
- 2 large Bananas
- 1 ½ cups Vegan Vanilla Frozen Yogurt

INSTRUCTIONS

1. Place almond milk, rum, creme de cacao, banana liqueur and bananas in a blender. Blend until smooth.
2. Add vegan frozen yogurt and continue to blend until mixture is smooth.
3. Pour and enjoy!

Strawberry Gin Milkshake

INGREDIENTS
- 1 1/4 oz. Dry Gin
- 4 scoops of Vegan Vanilla Ice Cream
- 1/4 cup of Strawberries
- 3 leaves of Fresh Basil
- Vegan Whipped Cream and Strawberries (as garnish)

INSTRUCTIONS

1. Chill two glasses.
2. Put gin, vegan vanilla ice cream, strawberries and basil in a blender and mix until smooth.
3. Garnish with vegan whipped cream and strawberry.

Peanut Butter Cup Smoothie

INGREDIENTS
- 1 frozen Banana
- 2 teaspoons unsweetened Cocoa Powder
- 2 tablespoons Powdered Peanut Butter
- ½ cup unsweetened Vanilla Almond Milk
- ¼ cup Dairy-free Yogurt
- 3-4 Ice cubes

INSTRUCTIONS

1. Put all ingredients in a blender and blend until smooth.

Mock Sangria (NON – ALCOHOLIC)

INGREDIENTS
- Chopped mix of Apples, Oranges, Lemons, & Strawberries
- 1/2 cup Red Grape Juice
- 1/2 cup Cranberry Juice
- 1/2 cup Orange Juice
- 1 1/2 cups Carbonated Water

INSTRUCTIONS

1. Add desired amount of chopped fruit to a large pitcher and fill it approx. 1/3 way.
2. Pour the juice and carbonated water into pitcher and gently stir.
3. Serve and enjoy!

Mauby Bark Drink

INGREDIENTS

- 1/2 cup Mauby Bark
- 3 cups light Brown Sugar
- 1/2 tbsp Fennel/Anise Seeds
- 1 stick Cinnamon (3″)
- 1 Star Anise
- 1 liter Water
- 1 tsp Angostura Bitters (optional)

INSTRUCTIONS

1. Add bark, star anise, fennel/anise seed, cinnamon, water and sugar to a medium pan. Place over medium-high heat.
2. Boil for 10-15 mins.
3. Turn off heat. Allow the syrup to cool.
4. Strain syrup into an airtight jar.
5. Taste syrup before straining. For stronger Mauby flavor, add a little more bark to syrup and boil for an additional 5 mins. Allow to cool again. For lighter Mauby flavor, dilute the syrup with some water.
6. Optional. To enhance flavor, add a few drops of Kola Champagne essence and Anise

Jamaican Sorrel

INGREDIENTS

- 2 cups Dried Sorrel OR Dried Hibiscus
- 1 Orange Peel
- 6 cups Water
- 1 cup Sugar, to taste
- 2 Cinnamon Sticks
- 2 inches of Ginger, sliced thin for mild flavor, chopped for stronger flavor

INSTRUCTIONS

1. Add all ingredients to a pot, bring to a gentle simmer, and cover for approx. 10 mins.
2. Check mixture and stir. Simmer for another 30 mins.
3. Remove from heat to cool. Refrigerate overnight for a stronger flavor.
4. Strain mixture. Add ice, water, and rum.
5. Mix and serve.

Barbados

Bajan Macaroni

INGREDIENTS
- 12 oz Macaroni
- 1 tbsp Vegan Butter
- 1 tbsp Olive Oil
- 1 Vegan Egg
- 1 cup of Almond Milk
- 1 medium White Onion, finely diced
- 2 tsp Yellow Mustard
- 2 tbsp Ketchup
- 1 tsp White Pepper
- 1 tsp Salt
- 16 oz Vegan Cheddar Cheese, grated
- ½ tsp Cayenne Pepper
- ½ tsp dry Ginger
- ½ Sweet Red Pepper, minced
- Panko Breadcrumbs
- 4 tbsp of Vegan Cheddar Cheese, grated

INSTRUCTIONS

1. Preheat oven to 350 degrees F.
2. Bring pot of salted water to a boil. Add macaroni. Cook for approx. 8 mins. until slightly tender (macaroni will continue to cook in oven). Strain.
3. Melt vegan butter and add oil in pan to then sauté the onion and red pepper until they soften.
4. In a bowl, whisk vegan eggs, almond milk, mustard, ketchup and seasonings until smooth.
5. Add macaroni, sauteed peppers and onion, and vegan grated cheese to bowl. Mix.
6. Place macaroni mix into a greased pan or casserole dish. Add panko breadcrumbs and grated vegan cheese to top of dish.
7. Bake for appox. 30-45 minutes or until entire dish is hot / cooked. Once you see it is brown and bubbling that should indicate it is done.

Johnny Cakes

INGREDIENTS

- 1 tsp Baking Powder
- 1 tsp Sea Salt
- 1 large Vegan Egg, lightly beaten
- 1 tbsp Vegan Butter, unsalted
- 1/2 cup All-purpose Flour
- 1 cup Cornmeal
- 2 tbsp granulated Sugar
- Cooking spray
- 1 1/2 cups Soy Milk
- Syrup or Vegan Butter, to top

INSTRUCTIONS

1. In a bowl, add flour, cornmeal, sugar, baking powder, and salt. Whisk until smooth.
2. In a small pot, place soy milk and vegan butter on medium-low heat to simmer.
3. Add Just egg, and hot milk and butter to the dry mix. Whisk.
4. Let batter sit for 10 mins.
5. In a large nonstick griddle or skillet, cover with cooking spray put on medium heat until hot.
6. Place 2 tablespoons of batter per johnnycake onto the pan and spread to about 3 inches in diameter, leaving a few inches of space in between each.
7. Cook until golden brown on both sides, 5-6 mins. on each side.
8. Repeat steps 5-7 until batter is finished, spraying the pan with a coating of cooking oil between batches. Should make approx. 20 cakes.
9. Top with butter or syrup, your choice.

CHAPTER 4

Cuba

Ropa Vieja

INGREDIENTS
- 2 large Oyster Mushrooms
- 1 tbsp Soy Sauce
- 1 tsp Oregano
- 1 Sazon Packet
- 1 tsp Adobo
- ¼ tsp Cumin
- ½ tsp Paprika
- ⅛ tsp Allspice
- ½ Lemon juice
- 1 sliced Red Bell Pepper
- 1 sliced green bell pepper
- ½ diced White Onion
- 2 minced Cloves Garlic
- Salt and Pepper to taste
- 1 tbsp Olive Oil
- 1 tbsp dry White Cooking Wine
- 1 tsp Tomato Paste
- 2 sliced Pimiento Stuffed Olives
- 2 Bay Leaves

INSTRUCTIONS

1. Cut mushrooms into four pieces. Place to the side.
2. Place all remaining ingredients in bowl and let it sit to marinate for 15 mins.
3. Cook mushrooms over medium heat in a large pot, frequently press down with a spatula to create a meatier texture.
4. Once mushroom is crispy on both sides, add the marinade to the pot.
5. Cook until the mixture has reached a boil, then lower heat and cover with lid.
6. Cook until most of the liquid is evaporated and serve with rice or quinoa.

Vegan Picadillo

INGREDIENTS
- 1 tbsp Neutral Cooking Oil OR Water/ Veggie Broth)
- ½ Yellow Onion, diced
- ¼ of a Red, Yellow, and Green Bell Pepper, diced
- ½ bunch chopped Cilantro, separate stems and leaves
- 3 cloves Garlic, finely sliced
- 6-10 pitted Green Olives, halves
- 3 tbsp Tomato Paste
- 1 cube of Vegan Beef-Flavored Bouillon
- ½ tbsp Badia's Sazon Tropical
- 1 tsp Cumin
- 1 tsp Salt-Free Seasoning Blend
- ½ tsp Oregano
- ¼ cup Water
- 11 oz Beyond Beef Crumbles, frozen

INSTRUCTIONS

1. Add oil to large pan and put on medium heat.
2. Add onion, bell peppers, and cilantro stems to pan. Sauté until tender, then add garlic and sauté for an additional 1-2 mins.
3. Add tomato paste and beef-flavored Bouillon cube to the pan. Mix until smooth.
4. Add all the spices to tomato paste mixture, then sauté for an additional minute.
5. Add water to the pan and bring the mixture to a simmer on medium-high heat for 3-5 mins.
6. Add in Beyond Beef Crumbles. Mix until well blended and cook for an additional 5-7 minutes, until crumbles thaw and cook.
7. Stir in green olives and cilantro leaves.
8. Serve.

TIP: You can also substitute the "beef" with 3 cups of cooked green lentils if you do not have access to alternative vegan "meat".

Dominica

Dominican Callaloo Soup

INGREDIENTS
- 2 lbs Young Dasheen OR Tannia Leaves OR Spinach
- 2-3 packs Vegan Crab Meat
- 1 cup Coconut Milk
- 1 large Onion
- 1 tbsp Oil
- 5 cups Water
- 1 tbsp Celery, chopped
- 1 tbsp Thyme, chopped
- 4 blades Chive, chopped
- 1 Hot Pepper
- 2 tbsp Salt
- 6 cloves Garlic, chopped
- Garlic powder, to taste
- 1 tbsp Black Pepper
- 1½ tbsp Turmeric
- 10 small Dumplings (dough made with spelt flour, salt & water)

INSTRUCTIONS

1. Boil vegan crabs in a large pot with salt and garlic powder. This should not take as long to boil as real crab meat.
2. Wash and peel outer skin from dasheen or tannia leaves. If using spinach, wash and chop leaves. Boil in 3 cups of water and 1/2 tablespoon of salt.
3. Add oil to a separate large pot on medium heat.
4. Stir in onion, celery and chopped garlic and sauté for 3 minutes.
5. Pour coconut milk and remaining 2 cups of water into the pot with sauteed onion, celery, and garlic.
6. Add dasheen/ tannia leaves or spinach leaves.
7. With blender (preferably handheld), pulse leaves mixture in the pot for approx. 15 secs.
8. Add thyme and hot pepper, dumplings, and boiled crabs.
9. Season with salt and black pepper.
10. Cover pot and let simmer for about 45 minutes.
11. Once cooked it can be served with quinoa, white rice or spelt bread.

Mountain Chick'n

INGREDIENTS
Mountain Chick'n
- Vegan Frog Legs
- 3 tbsp Lime or Lemon juice
- 2 tsp Salt
- 2 cloves Garlic
- 1 tsp Black Pepper
- 1 tsp Vinegar
- 1 tsp Thyme, chopped
- 1 Green Pepper, sliced
- 1 cup Flour
- 1 cup grapeseed oil, for frying

Gravy
- 1 tbsp Vegan Butter
- 1 small Onion, sliced
- 1 cup Water
- 1 tbsp Flour

Provisions
- 2 Green Figs/ Plantains, sliced
- 2 Dasheen Taro root, cut into 4 pieces
- 2 Yams, cut into 4 piece

INSTRUCTIONS
Mountain Chick'n

1. Season vegan frog legs with salt, garlic, pepper, vinegar, thyme and let sit for 1-2 hours.
2. Pat vegan frog legs dry with paper towels.
3. Coat vegan frog legs in flour.
4. Heat vegetable oil in a frying pan until very hot.
5. Place vegan frog legs in the hot oil and fry until golden brown, turning over as necessary.

Provisions

1. Peel and clean provisions (Green fig/banana, Dasheen, Yam).
2. Boil or steam provisions until tender, but firm

Gravy

1. Melt 1 tbsp Vegan butter in a saucepan.
2. Add sliced onion. Sauté for approx. 1 min.
3. Add 1 cup of water and bring to a boil.
4. Gradually stir in flour to thicken the gravy and simmer on medium heat for approx. 5 mins.
5. Add the vegan frog legs to the pot of gravy, stir and simmer for another 2 minutes.
6. Serve the Mountain Chick'n with the provisions, and a green salad!

BBQ Seitan

INGREDIENTS

Dry Ingredients
- 3 cups Vital Wheat Gluten
- 1 cup Nutritional Yeast Flakes
- ¼ cup Basil
- ¼ cup Cumin
- ¼ cup Paprika
- ¼ cup Oregano

Wet Ingredients
- 1-2 cups of favorite veggies such as Carrots, Celery, Onions, Bell Pepper, finely chopped
- ½ cup Soy Sauce
- 6 oz. (1 small can) Tomato Paste
- 2 tbsp Mustard
- 3 cups Water

BBQ Sauce
- 1 cup Tomato Paste
- 1 cup Ketchup
- 1/2 cup Tamari Soy Sauce
- 3/4 cup Molasses or Maple Syrup
- 1/4 cup Water, to desired thickness
- Dash of Hot Sauce or Cayenne Pepper, to taste

INSTRUCTIONS

1. Preheat oven to 350°F.
2. Use food processor or finely chop vegetables. Place all wet ingredients in pot and simmer 10 mins. --- Other method: Sautée veggies with oil 10 mins, especially if using mushrooms, then add the other wet ingredients; use water heated to warm.
3. Separately, mix all dry ingredients.
4. Mix simmered wet ingredients and dry ingredients until blended thoroughly, you want it to all be wet. If mixture is too watery, gradually add more VWG until more dough like. Gradually add water if mixture is too dry.
5. Knead and fold the mixture for about 2 minutes.
6. Place enough aluminum foil on a baking sheet to cover and wrap the seitan as a large loaf.
7. Place the seitan to the middle of the foil and shape to a big rectangle, approx. 9×12” and 1” high.
8. Bake for appox. 45 mins. per side.
9. Cool for appox. 20 mins. and remove from foil before slicing.
10. Sautée to crisp up to serve on sandwiches, stir-fry recipes, or can be baked.
11. Stores in refrigerator up to 10 days.

Dominican Republic

Traditional Dominican Breakfast

INGREDIENTS

Sweet Mangú
- 3 Yellow or Green Plantains
- 3 tbsp Vegan Butter
- 1/2 tsp Salt
- 1/2 tsp Garlic Powder
- 1/2 tsp Onion Powder

Vegan Scrambled Eggs
- 8 tbsp Vegan Egg
- 2 cups ice cold Water
- 2 tsp no salt Adobo Seasoning
- 1 tsp Salt
- 1/2 cup Onion, diced
- 1/2 cup Green Bell Pepper, diced
- 1 tbsp Vegan Butter

Fried Vegan Cheese
- 1 block Follow Your Heart Mozzarella Style Vegan Cheese, sliced ¼ inch thick
- 1/4 cup Corn Starch or Arrowroot Starch
- 1/4 cup Avocado oil or refined Coconut oil

Fried Vegan Salami
- 4 slices Vegan Salami
- Refined Coconut oil spray

INSTRUCTIONS
Sweet Mangú

1. Slice the plantains into thirds, place in pot and add enough water to cover over plantains.
2. Bring to a boil for 10-30 mins. or until soft.
3. Remove plantains from water.
4. Peel and mash/ blend plantains with food processor.
5. Add vegan butter, salt, garlic powder and onion powder into the plantain blend and mix until it's smooth. Add water if the mangú isn't getting creamy when mixing.
6. Top the mangú with pickled red onions.

Vegan Scrambled Eggs

1. In a bowl whisk vegan egg, cold water, adobo and salt until smooth. Set aside.
2. Heat a pan over medium heat and melt vegan butter.
3. Add onions and pepper to pan. Cook until they are tender.
4. Add vegan egg mixture to the pan and stir slowly until the vegan egg mix hardens and begins to form solid. Continue to stir/ mix scrambled eggs until they are no longer in liquid form.
5. Remove from the pan once cooked thoroughly.

Fried Vegan Cheese

1. Add oil to frying pan and place over medium heat until it is hot.
2. In a bowl add corn starch.
3. Cover each slice of vegan mozzarella cheese in corn starch and add them to the hot pan, cooking each side for approx. 3 mins. on each side until it turns golden brown.
4. Place on plate with paper towel placed over it to absorb any excess oil.

Fried Vegan Salami

1. Heat a pan over medium high heat.
2. Lightly spray the pan with the coconut oil. Add vegan salami slices.
3. Cook for 3 mins. on each side or until lightly brown.

Tostones (Fried Green Plantains)

INGREDIENTS
- 4 green plantains
- 1 cup vegetable or canola oil, or as needed
- 2 cups water
- 4 cloves garlic, minced
- 1 tablespoon salt, plus more to top
- Juice of 1 lime
- Mojo Verde or other sauce, to dip

INSTRUCTIONS

1. Cut and peel each plantain, keeping inner plantain intact.
2. Cut the plantains into sliced pieces, about 1″ thick.
3. Fill a large skillet about a third of the way with oil. Heat over medium for a few minutes to warm up the oil until warm.
4. In a large bowl, combine water, garlic, salt, and lime juice. Set aside.
5. Add the plantain slices to the oil. The oil should be just hot enough that it begins to lightly bubble shortly after adding the plantains. Fry the plantains until softened and golden.
6. Place plantains to a plate lined with paper towel to absorb any excess oil.
7. Using the bottom of a glass, or large spoon gently flatten each fried plantain piece. Press down enough to flatten but be careful not to break apart.
8. Dip plantain in the garlic-lime water. Let it sit for about 5-10 secs., then remove and gently pat dry with a paper towel. Repeat with all pieces of plantain.
9. Heat oil over medium-high heat. Add plantains back to the oil in batches and briefly fry to crisp, appox. 1 min. Remove and transfer to a paper towel lined plate.
10. Sprinkle lightly with salt and dip in chosen sauce.

Grenada

Oil Down with Yucca

INGREDIENTS

- 3-4, approx. 2 lbs. Cassava
- 3 Carrots, chopped
- 2 stalks Celery, chopped
- 1 Onion, chopped
- Vegetable oil
- 1 tbsp Curry powder
- 1 Habanero Pepper, for spice
- 30 oz, about 3 ½ cups Coconut milk
- 2 cups Water
- Salt
- Pepper
- 3 handfuls Spinach
- 1 recipe Spinners or Sinkers

INSTRUCTIONS

1. Sauté the onions, carrots, and celery in oil until softened and slightly browned.
2. Add curry and hot pepper. Cut pepper in half if you want to make it extra spicy.
3. Add coconut milk, yucca, and water.
4. Simmer uncovered for appox. 30 mins., then add spinach.
5. Add dumplings. Stir and cook until the stew is thick, and dumplings are fully cooked.

Haiti

Haitian Griot (Fried Jackfruit)

INGREDIENTS
Jackfruit
- 1 Lbs. (12oz) Young Green Jackfruit in brine
- ½ Cup Haitian Epis
- 1 teaspoon Cumin
- 2 teaspoon Sea Salt
- 1 teaspoon Paprika
- 1 teaspoon Black Pepper
- Oil For Deep Frying About ½ Quart (or more if needed)

Coating
- 2 tablespoon Cornstarch
- 1 Cup All-Purpose Flour

Sauce
- 1 tablespoon Red Pepper Flakes
- ¼ Cup Red Bell Peppers Sliced
- 2 tablespoon Olive Oil
- ¼ Cup Chopped Onions
- 1 tablespoon Apple Cider Vinegar

INSTRUCTIONS
Haitian Griot / Fried Jackfruit

1. Drain and remove jackfruit to place into a bowl.
2. Add Haitian seasoning. Mix well.
3. Add remaining ingredients and mix well.
4. Cover and marinate for approx. 30 mins. or more.
5. In a separate bowl, mix cornstarch and flour. Set aside.
6. Take jackfruit pieces and coat in the flour mixture.
7. Heat oil to a hot temperature. Approx. 400°
8. Transfer jackfruit pieces to oil. Be careful not to get burned from oil splatter.
9. Deep fry until golden. Remove and place cooked pieces to a plate covered with paper towel to capture any excess oil.

Sauce for Coating

1. Using medium size bowl, add peppers, oil, green onions, and vinegar. Mix well and coat pieces of fried jackfruit.

Bahamian Conch Salad

INGREDIENTS
- 8 ounces baked Tofu, diced
- Juice of 3 Limes
- Juice of 1 Navel Orange
- 1 Red Bell Pepper, diced
- 1 Orange Bell Pepper, diced
- 1 Yellow Bell Pepper, diced
- ½ Scotch Bonnet Pepper, finely chopped
- ½ White Onion, diced
- Salt and Pepper, to taste

INTRUCTIONS

1. Combine peppers, onions, tofu, lime juice and orange juice in a medium size mixing bowl. Toss together until evenly mixed.
2. Let salad marinate in refrigerator until cold.
3. Serve and enjoy!

Jamaica

"Oxtail" & Butter Bean

INGREDIENTS
- 1 large dark Mushroom
- I Bell Pepper
- Celery
- Tomato Paste
- 1 cup Black Eye Peas
- 1 cup Lentil Peas
- 1 can Butter Beans
- 1 tbsp Salt
- 1 tbsp fresh Garlic
- 1 tbsp of All-purpose Seasoning
- 1 tbsp Black Pepper
- 1 cup of Bean Flour
- 1 tbsp Garlic powder
- 1 tbsp. Onion powder
- 1 tbsp Oxtail Seasoning
- 1/2 tbsp of All Spice
- 2 Stalks Scallion
- Thyme
- 1 Hot Pepper
- 1 tbsp Vinegar
- Coconut oil
- 1 ½ tsp Browning

INSTRUCTIONS

1. Cook lentil beans and blackeye peas until tender.
2. Mix lentil beans and blackeye peas in large bowl.
3. Add onion powder, garlic powder, black pepper, seasoned salt, salt and oxtail seasoning.
4. Place mushrooms in bean flour and browning.
5. Mix until compacted.
6. Place plastic wrap on table and add some bean flour to cover plastic wrap.
7. Place mixture in center of plastic wrap.
8. Grab plastic wrap, fold it up on both ends to cover the top of mixture with flour as well.
9. Place a piece of celery in the middle of mixture and push it down until it's all the way through the mixture. Cut end of celery stick to shorten closer to mixture.
10. Fold plastic wrap tightly around mixture. Place in refrigerator for 24hrs.
11. Remove from refrigerator and unwrap, slice it all the way down in pieces.
12. In a pan, place heat 2 teaspoons of coconut oil. Make sure not to burn oil.
13. Place your mixture on pan and cook until golden-brown color on both sides.
14. Remove "oxtail".
15. Using same oil, add garlic, thyme, scallion, onion, hot pepper, and vinegar to pan. Stir.
16. Add half cup of water, ½ teaspoon of browning, oxtail seasoning, and tomato paste. Stir.
17. Raise to a medium heat. Place "oxtail" back in pan.
18. Add butter beans and cover pan. Simmer for approx. 15mins.

Ackee and "Saltfish"

INGREDIENTS
Vegan "Saltfish"
- 1 can 14 oz of Hearts of Palm
- 1 cup filtered Water
- 1 tbsp Sea Salt
- 2 tsp Kelp or Nori Flakes, optional

Ackee
- 1 lb cooked Ackee or canned Ackee
- 2 tbsp Coconut Oil
- 4 Garlic Cloves, finely sliced
- 2 Plum Tomatoes, chopped
- 1 medium sized Bell Pepper, chopped
- ½ Red Onion, chopped
- 3-4 stalks fresh Thyme, remove stems
- ¼ tbsp Scotch bonnet, or to taste
- 3 stalks Scallion, slice
- Sea Salt, to taste
- Black pepper, to taste

INSTRUCTIONS
Vegan "Saltfish"

1. Remove Hearts of Palm and cut each piece in half pieces, then slightly shred them.
2. In a mason jar, add hearts of palm, a cup of water, and tablespoon of salt which is your salt brine. Stir lightly.
3. Add kelp flakes if you want a fishy taste. Set aside and sit for a minimum of 30 mins.
4. Heat approx. 1 tbsp of coconut oil in a pan (add more if needed).
5. Add garlic, tomatoes, bell peppers, onions and cook until soft.
6. Add thyme and stir for approx. 1-2 mins.
7. Drain off the salt brine of Hearts of Palm, rinse well, and pat dry.
8. Raise the heat a little and add Hearts of Palm to pan.
9. Stir and cook until Hearts of Palm crisp up a bit for approx. 5 mins.
   Ackee
10. Drain ackee and add to pan. Stir gently to not break ackee apart.
11. Add a some more salt and black pepper to taste.
12. Remove from heat and serve with a side dish such as callaloo/ spinach, breadfruit or fried plantain.

Curried "Goat" Stew

INGREDIENTS

"Goat"

- 1 package Upton's Naturals Seitan, original
- ¼ cup Tamari Soy Sauce
- 1 Tbs. Jamaican curry powder
- 4 cloves Garlic, minced
- 1 tsp Black Pepper
- 1 tsp ground Cumin
- 1 tsp dried Oregano
- 1 tsp dried Thyme
- ¼ tsp Allspice
- A pinch of Red Pepper Flakes
- Water
- Vegetable oil

Stew

- 2 tbs Vegetable oil
- 1 large Onion, diced
- 2 Bell Peppers, chopped
- 3 large Potatoes, chunks
- 6 cloves Garlic, minced
- 1 Chile Pepper, minced
- 3 tbs Jamaican Curry powder
- 2 tsp dried Thyme
- ½ tsp Black Pepper
- Salt, to taste
- 1-15 oz. can Diced Tomatoes
- Vegetable broth OR Water
- Fresh Parsley, chopped

INSTRUCTIONS

1. Cut seitan into small chunks and place in a bowl.
2. Add tamari, cumin, oregano, thyme, allspice, red pepper flakes, curry powder, garlic cloves, and black pepper,
3. Add water so that marinade covers the seitan. Marinate for a minimum of 30 min. or more to soak flavor.
4. Remove seitan from marinade and pat dry.
5. Heat oil in a deep depth sauté pan over medium-high heat.
6. Add the seitan to the oil and cook until browned on all sides.
7. Transfer to plate covered with paper towel and continue until all the seitan is browned. Set aside.
8. Sauté the onion and bell peppers for approx. 5 mins. until they start to soften. Add more oil to the pan if needed.
9. Add potatoes to the pan and cook for about 3-4 mins. or until they brown.
10. Add garlic, chile pepper, curry powder, thyme, black pepper, and salt. Stir evenly.
11. Add diced tomatoes. Stir.
12. Place seitan back in pan and add water/ broth to cover the potatoes.
13. Bring the liquid to a boil, and then reduce the heat to low.
14. Cover and simmer the stew for approx. 15 mins. or until potatoes are soft.
15. Uncover the pot to allow sauce to thicken for approx. 5 mins.
16. Garnish with parsley. You can serve over a side of quinoa or rice.

St. Kitts & Nevis

Black Pudding

INGREDIENTS
- 8 oz Black Beans, cooked & mashed
- 3 oz Mushrooms, chopped
- 2 oz Oats, used for porridge
- 1 oz Textured Vegetable Protein
- 1 Red Onion, finely chopped
- 2 cloves Garlic, crushed
- 4 oz Vegetable Stock
- ½ tbsp Virgin Olive oil
- 1 tbsp Tamarind paste
- 1 tbsp Soy Sauce
- 1 tbsp Parsley
- 1 tbsp Thyme
- ½ tbsp Black Pepper

INSTRUCTIONS

1. Place textured vegetable protein into vegetable stock in a bowl, cover, and let sit for 1 hr.
2. Sautee onion and garlic in oil until soft.
3. Add mushrooms, and cook for about 10-15 min, then remove from heat.
4. Strain the soaked textured vegetable protein and press out any excess liquid.
5. Add textured vegetable protein to pan along with remaining ingredients.
6. Place mixture into a non-stick square pan. For best results use 7in. pan.
7. Press down firmly, cover, and place in refrigerator for 2 hrs.
8. Lightly spread with olive oil, then bake at 400` for approx. 35-40 mins. until browned.

St. Lucia

Green Fig Salad

INGREDIENTS

- 6 Green Figs OR Green Bananas, boiled, peeled, & sliced
- 2 Sweet Red Peppers, chopped
- 1 cup of mixed Broad Beans/ Peas, & Carrots, chopped
- ½ Red Onion, sliced thinly
- 2 Scallions, sliced
- 1 tsp of Mustard powder
- ½ cup of Vegan Mayonnaise
- ½ tbsp. of Thyme
- ½ tsp of Black Pepper
- 1 tsp of Garlic, granules
- Sea Salt, to taste

INSTRUCTIONS

1. Boil carrot and beans/peas on high heat in saucepan with some water until tender.
2. Strain water and set aside with figs until cooled off.
3. Place figs, beans/peas, carrots and red peppers in a large bowl.
4. Add vegan mayonnaise, red onions, and scallion. Mix until evenly coated.
5. Add mustard powder, thyme, black pepper, garlic and salt to taste. Mix thoroughly.
6. Enjoy.

St. Vincent & the Grenadines

Madongo Dumplings

INGREDIENTS
- 1lb Madungo, cassava starch
- ½ cup Coconut, grated
- ¼ tsp Nutmeg, grated
- ¼ cup Easy Bake flour, optional
- Pinch of Salt
- Cinnamon, to taste
- Brown Sugar, to taste
- Water
- Banana leaf

INSTRUCTIONS

1. Boil water in pot.
2. Wet madungo with a little water and form into a ball.
3. Place the madungo ball into boiling water for about 2-3 mins. or until the outside is a "Glue-like" looking texture.
4. Remove the ball from the pot and place it in a container to mash.
5. Using a spoon peel the outside "glue-like" skin from the ball. Mash ball while hot.
6. Warm banana leaf over fire, wrap portions in the banana leaf, and bake in an iron pot, or skillet.
7. Remove the banana leaf when slightly cooked to give crunch.

Roasted Breadfruit

INGREDIENTS
- 1 fully mature breadfruit
- 1 tsp oil

INSTRUCTIONS

1. Preheat oven 425` F.
2. Cut around the stem of breadfruit and about 1 in. deep and remove.
3. Cut an 'X' shape on the base of the fruit, this will help greatly to cook the breadfruit.
4. Rub cooking oil over the breadfruit skin. Wrap breadfruit securely with tin foil. You can also wrap in parchment paper and then wrap it in tin foil over the paper.
5. Place in the oven and bake for approx. 1 ½ - 2 hrs.
6. Remove breadfruit from oven and allow to cool.
7. Peel breadfruit while still hot/warm but cool enough to hold, cut breadfruit in half, and then remove the core by cutting it out.
8. Slice and enjoy.

"Fish" Sticks with Tartar Sauce

INGREDIENTS

"Fish" Sticks
- 20 oz can of Jackfruit, in water
- 1 tbsp Lemon Juice
- 1/4 cup Vegan Mayonnaise
- 1/2 tsp French's Dijon Mustard, make sure no dairy
- 1/4 cup Panko Breadcrumbs
- 1 tsp Old Bay Seasoning
- 1/2 tsp Salt
- pinch Sugar
- 1 tbsp Oil

Tartar Sauce
- 1/4 cup Vegan Mayonnaise
- 1 tbsp Dill Pickles finely chopped
- 1 1/2 tsp White Wine Vinegar
- 1/2 tsp Mustard
- Salt, to taste
- Pepper, to taste

INSTRUCTIONS

1. Drain and rinse jackfruit. Shredded in food processor.
2. Add lemon juice, vegan mayonnaise, dijon mustard, Old Bay Seasoning, salt, sugar to food processor.
3. In a plate, add breadcrumbs some Old Bay Seasoning. Mix.
4. Make balls out of mixture and fully coat in breadcrumbs.
5. Shape into "fish stick" shape.
6. Add oil to a non-stick pan and place heat on medium-high heat.
7. Place fish sticks on to pan. Cook until golden and crisp all around.
8. Mix all ingredients for tartar sauce.
9. Dip and enjoy.

Trinidad & Tobago

Vegan Chick'n Pelau

INGREDIENTS
- 2 lbs Vegan Chicken, cut into small pieces
- 3 tbsp Green Seasoning, or seasoning you use to season your chicken
- 5 tbsp Brown Sugar
- 2 cups Wild Rice
- 1/2 cup Onion, chopped
- 1/2 cup Pimento Pepper, chopped
- 2 cloves Garlic, chopped
- 2 tbsp Parsley, chopped
- 2 tbsp Cilantro, chopped
- 2 tbsp Ginger, chopped
- 1/2 cup Pumpkin, cubed
- 2 cans (30 oz) canned Pigeon Peas or 1 3/4 lbs fresh
- 2 tbsp Salt
- 2 cups Coconut Milk
- 2 cups hot Water
- 1 tbsp Ketchup
- 2 tsp Black Pepper

INSTRUCTIONS

1. Season vegan chicken with green seasoning and set aside.
2. Heat a heavy pot and add sugar, sprinkling evenly at the bottom of the pan.
3. Allow sugar to heat until it caramelizes, or all sugar is brown.
4. Add seasoned chicken, stirring vegan chicken into sugar browning. Cook for approx. 5 mins.
5. Drain and add pigeon peas. Stir and cook for about 5 mins.
6. Add rice to pot. Add more water if needed to cook the rice properly. Stir.
7. Add coconut milk, water, pumpkin, parsley, peppers, onion, garlic, ginger, salt, black pepper, and ketchup to pot. Stir.
8. Bring pot to boil, then reduce heat to simmer for approx. 30 mins. or until rice is partially cooked.
9. Add cilantro.
10. Steam until rice is cooked fully and ready to serve.

Roti

INGREDIENTS
•1 ½ cups spelt flour or whole-wheat flour, plus more for rolling
•½ teaspoon salt
2 tablespoons extra-virgin olive oil, divided
1/4 cup plus 1 tablespoon water, plus more as needed

INSTRUCTIONS

1. Combine flour and salt in a large bowl. Add 1 tablespoon oil and mix with your fingers until crumbly.
2. Slowly add water and mix until dough comes together. If dough doesn't come together, mix in a little more water.
3. Knead on lightly floured surface until dough is smooth and no longer sticks to your fingers, about 2 minutes. Cover with a plastic wrap; let rest for 15 – 30 mins.
4. Divide the dough into 8 balls and cover with plastic wrap.
5. Lightly flour rolling pin and on a clean work surface, flatten 1 dough ball and roll it out, picking it up and rotating it to make sure it doesn't stick to counter. Flatten until very thin and approx. 5 inches in diameter.
6. Transfer to lightly floured baking sheet and loosely cover with plastic wrap.
7. Repeat with the remaining dough, spacing the breads on baking sheets so they don't touch.
8. Heat a large cast-iron skillet, heavy skillet or griddle over medium-high heat. Add one dough and cook until bubbles lightly appear, approx. 30sec.- 1 min. Flip, then brush the top side with a little oil and cook until lightly puffed, 30 secs. – 1 min.
9. Transfer to a plate and cover with foil to keep warm. Repeat with remaining dough, stacking and covering them to keep warm.

CHAPTER 14

Bonus Traditional Dishes

Guyanese Pepper Pot

INGREDIENTS

- 1 pack Extra-Firm Tofu, cubed
- 1 pack Farm Boy Vegan Beef, thawed & mixed.
- 1 large White Onion, peeled & chopped
- 5 cloves Garlic, finely sliced
- 1 Sweet Potato OR Yuca, skinned & cubed
- 2 medium Carrots, sliced
- ½ pack / bunch fresh Thyme, leave on stem
- 5 Cloves
- 2 Cinnamon Sticks, whole
- 1 whole Scotch Bonnet, cut to increase spice
- 1 pack Vegan Sausage, sliced
- 1/3 cup Sea Salt
- 2-3 100 ml bottle of Guyanese Pride Cassareep
- 2-4 leaves Basil, whole leaves

INSTRUCTIONS

1. Place oil in large pot at medium heat. Sautee onions and garlic until lightly browned.
2. Add carrots, sweet potato/ yuca. Cook for approx. 7-10 mins.
3. Add tofu, vegan beef, and vegan sausage. Stir and cook for 5-10 mins.
4. Add cassareep to the pot. Add enough water to cover the ingredients.
5. Add cinnamon sticks, basil leaves, cloves, thyme, hot peppers, and salt. Cut pepper to increase spice in dish. Bring to a boil.
6. Reduce heat and cook on low for 2-3 hours.
7. Serve in a bowl.

Puerto Rican Arroz Con Gandules

INGREDIENTS

- 2 tbsp Neutral Cooking Oil OR Water OR Veggie Broth
- ½ Yellow Onion, diced
- ¼ each Red, Yellow, Green Peppers, diced
- 3 cloves of Garlic, minced
- 2 tbsp Tomato Paste
- 1 cube of Vegan Chicken-Flavored Bouillon
- 2 tsp Capers
- 2 Bay Leaves
- 1 tsp Salt-Free Seasoning Blend
- 1 tsp Cumin
- ½ tbsp Badia's Sazon Tropical
- 1 tsp Goya's Sazon con Azafran
- 2 tbsp Tamari Soy Sauce
- 1 15.5 oz can Guandules Secos, Dry Pigeon Peas, with liquid
- 1 13.5 oz can full-Fat Coconut Milk
- 2 cup White Rice
- 1 bunch Cilantro, coarsely chopped
- Black Pepper, to taste
- Oregano, to taste

INSTRUCTIONS

1. Place cooking oil in a medium pot on medium-high heat.
2. Add the onion, bell peppers, ½ a bunch of cilantro, bay leaves, and garlic to the pot. Sauté until the onions are translucent for approx. 3-5 mins.
3. Add vegan chicken-flavored bouillon and tomato paste. Stir into the vegetables. Sauté for 2-3 mins.
4. Add the capers, can of guandules secos, tamari, cumin, and sazon con azafran. Stir evenly and sauté for approx. 3 mins.
5. Add ½ of remaining cilantro, coconut milk and remaining spices. Simmer on high heat.
6. Rinse rice and add to mixture. When rice starts to boil to top of pot, add the remaining cilantro, mix well.
7. Cover and reduce heat to low. Simmer for about 20 mins. until cooked.
8. Enjoy.

Honduras Plato Tipico

INGREDIENTS
"Meat"
- 450g Vegan Beef, sliced
- Vegan Pork, sliced in strips
- 4 Vegan Chorizo, sliced
- ½ tsp Salt
- ½ tsp Black Pepper
- 2 cloves Garlic
- 2 tbsp Olive Oil
- 3 tbsp Vinegar

Stewed Beans
- 2 cans Kidney Beans
- 1 Red Onion, thinly sliced
- 3 Bell Peppers, green, yellow & red, thinly sliced
- 2 cloves Garlic, mash or finely chopped
- 2 tbsp Olive Oil
- 1 tsp Oregano
- ¼ tsp Salt
- ¼ tsp White Pepper
- 1 pinch Cayenne Pepper
- ¼ tsp Thyme
- ¼ tsp Paprika
- 250ml Ketchup
- 250ml Water

Chismol
- 2 large Tomatoes
- 1 large Green Bell Pepper

- 1 Red Onion
- 3 sprigs Coriander
- ½ tsp Salt
- ½ tsp Black Pepper
- ¼ tsp Cumin
- 2 tbsp Lemon Juice

Fried Plantain

- 2 Plantains, ripe
- 4 tbsp Vegetable oil

Rice

- 200g Wild Rice
- 1 tbsp Green Bell Pepper, diced
- 1 tbsp Red Onion, diced
- 1 clove Garlic, thinly sliced
- ½ tsp Salt
- 1 tbsp Vegetable oil
- 500ml Wate

INSTRUCTIONS

1. Place vegan beef and sausage in bowl with salt, pepper, garlic, olive oil, and vinegar. Marinate for a minimum of one hr.
2. Place strips of vegan meat, vegan sausage, and vegan chorizo on grill and cook.

Stewed Beans

1. Heat the olive oil on medium-high heat in pot. Add onion, bell peppers and mashed garlic cloves. Sauté until tender.
2. Add beans. Stir and lower to a medium heat.
3. Add spices and ketchup. Mix thoroughly.
4. Add water and lower the heat to medium-low. Simmer for about 15 mins.

Chismol:

1. Mix vegetables, seasoning, and lemon juice.
   Plantains
2. Peel and cut plantain in half. Cut each half lengthwise into about 4 slices each
3. Heat vegetable oil on medium heat in frying pan. Place each slice in pan and cook until slightly browned on each side.
4. Remove and place to side.

Rice

1. On medium heat, add oil to pan. Add green bell pepper, onion, and garlic. Sauté for 2 mins.
2. Add rice and salt. Stir.
3. Add water and bring to a boil. Change heat to medium-low. Cover and simmer for about 20 min. or until rice is cooked.
4. Serve with other dishes and enjoy.

Ecuador Encebollado De Pescado

INGREDIENTS

- 2 lbs fresh Vegan Tuna
- 1 lb Yuca OR Cassava, fresh or frozen
- 2 tbs Sunflower oil
- 2 Tomatoes, diced
- ½ Red Onion, diced
- 1 tsp Chili powder
- 2 tsp ground Cumin
- 8 cups of Water
- 5 pieces of Cilantro
- Salt, to taste

Toppings
- Pickled Red Onion and Tomato Salsa
- Plantain chips
- Tostado corn nuts OR Popcorn

INSTRUCTIONS

1. Heat oil on medium. Add onion, tomato, cumin, chili powder and salt. Stir.
2. Add cilantro and water and bring to boil.
3. Add tuna, stir and cook for about 15 mins.
4. Strain tuna keeping broth to use later.
5. Mash vegan tuna into smaller sized pieces, if not already.
6. Using the saved broth, bring to a boil and add the yuca. Cook until tender but not too soft to break apart so easily, approx. 30-40 minutes.
7. Remove yuca from the broth. After removing strings, cut into small chunks.
8. Add yuca chunks and tuna into the broth over a low flame. Adjust seasonings if needed.
9. Serve with toppings of choice.

Belize Rice & Beans

INGREDIENTS
- 1 lb. Dry Kidney Beans
- 3 cups Rice
- 4 cloves Garlic, whole
- 4 cloves Garlic, crushed
- 5 large Onions, chopped
- 1 Green Pepper, diced
- 1stalk Celery chopped
- 1 ½ cup Bay Leaf
- 1 minced Parsley leaf
- 2 cans (400ml) Coconut Milk
- 4 tbsp Coconut oil
- 4 tbsp. Black Pepper
- ½ tsp Salt
- Water

INSTRUCTIONS

1. Soak the beans overnight. Drain and add to large pot, add beans.
2. Add enough water to cover the beans, 4 whole cloves of garlic and bring to a boil. Cook for about 1 hr or until soft.
3. In a separate pan, sauté crushed garlic, onions, celery, bay leaf, and green pepper with coconut oil.
4. Add sauté to pot with beans along with chopped parsley, salt and black pepper. Stir.
5. Add rice to pot along with coconut milk and coconut oil. Stir and adjust the salt if needed.
6. Cover and cook on medium-low heat for approx. 45 mins. or until the rice is cooked.
7. Serve alongside another favorite dish.

Ghana Cassava & Plantain Fufu

INGREDIENTS
- 10 ½ oz un-ripened Plantain
.• 16 oz Cassava
.• 1 ½ -2 cup Water, for blending
- 4 tbsp Water, for steaming
- 2 large Cassava
- 1 tbsp dairy-free Butter
- 1 tsp Salt
- 1 tsp Black Pepper

INSTRUCTIONS

1. Peel plantain and cut it into cubes.
2. Boil your cassava until soft for approx. 20-30 mins. Test with a sharp knife until it can go all the way through cassava. Strain and let cool.
3. Peel the cassava and cut into large chunks.
4. Peel and scrape the cassava, remove strings and cut into large chunks.
5. Place cassava and plantain into the blender. Add dairy-free butter and seasoning.
6. Add water. Use less if you want fufu to be firmer, or more water if you want softer.
7. Blend until smooth paste.
8. Heat saucepan on medium. Add blended mixture. Continue to stir for 8-10 mins to remove lumps. Texture should be slightly sticky.
9. Add remaining water to the mixture. Reduce the heat to low and steam for another 8-10 mins.
10. Raise back to medium heat and stir. The fufu might look too soft, but it will become firmer as it cools down.
11. Place fufu in bowl and add 1 tsp of water on the surface. Let cool.
12. Shape fufu into a ball and serve with soup or stew of your choice.
13. Serve with soup.

Ethiopian Seitan Chick'n Doro Wat

INGREDIENTS

- 1-1/2 to 2 pounds Chicken Style Seitan, cut small chunks
- 3 tbsp Lemon Juice
- 5 tbsp Vegan Butter
- 1 large Red Onion, quartered
- 1 large Yellow Onion, quartered
- 2 tbsp Olive Oil
- 1 tbsp Garlic, minced
- 1 tbsp Ginger, minced
- ⅓ cup Berbere Spice powder
- 1 ½ tsp Sea Salt
- ½ cup sweet Red Wine
- 1 cup Vegan Bouillon chicken flavored dissolved in 1 cup water

INSTRUCTIONS

1. Place 3 tbsp of vegan butter and olive oil in a large pot.
2. Add onion. Sauté, cover and cook on low heat for approx. 45 mins.
3. Place seitan chunks in large bowl and add lemon juice. Mix and let sit for a minimum of 30 min.
4. Add garlic and ginger. Stir. Cover and continue cooking for about 30 mins.
5. Add berbere seasoning and the 2 more tbsp vegan butter to pot. Stir. Cover and continue to cook for about 30 more mins.
6. Add seitan chunks, Bouillon broth and wine to pot and bring to a boil.
7. Reduce heat to low and cook for appox. 45 mins.
8. Adjust seasonings if needed. Simmer for 10-15 mins.
9. Remove from heat and serve over quinoa.

Panama Sancocho (Root Stew)

INGREDIENTS
- ¼ cup of Olive Oil
- 3 cloves Garlic, crushed
- 1 tspn Oregano leaves, dry
- 1 cup of yellow Split Peas
- 1qt Water
- 1qt Vegetable Broth
- 1 cup dry Porcini Mushrooms
- ¼ lb of Cassava, peeled & cut into small chunks
- ¼ lb of Malanga, optional
- ¼ lb of West Indian Pumpkin
- 1 unripe Plantain, cut into ½" slices
- ¼ lb of Yam, optional
- 1 Corn on the Cob, cut into ½" slices, optional
- 1 bunch of Cilantro, chopped
- 1 bunch Parsley, chopped
- 1½ tsp Salt, to taste
- ½ tsp Black Pepper, to taste

INSTRUCTIONS

1. To dry mushrooms, wash and pat-dry. Place on oiled baking pan, add a little salt and cook in the oven at 200` F for about 1 hr. Cut into small pieces. Set aside.
2. Heat the olive oil on medium heat in large pot. Add garlic, oregano, and split peas. Stir and let cook for a few seconds.
3. Add vegetable broth and water. Cover and simmer on low heat until split peas are soft. Add more water if it evaporates and stir.
4. Add dry mushrooms, cassava, malanga, plantain, pumpkin, yam, and corn. Cover pot.
5. Simmer over medium heat until all the vegetables are cooked.
6. Add cilantro and parsley.
7. Season with salt and pepper, to taste.
8. Serve with rice or quinoa.

Venezuela Shredded "Beef"

INGREDIENTS
- ½ Capsicum, cut in small cubes
- ½ White Onion, chopped
- 150g Oyster mushrooms, cut in strips
- 1 clove Garlic, minced
- 1 Tomato, grated
- ½ tsp Smoked Paprika
- ½ tsp Sweet Paprika
- ½ tsp Onion powder
- Salt, to taste
- Pepper, to taste
- Olive oil

INSTRUCTIONS

1. Place capsicum and onion in pan with a drizzle of olive oil on medium heat. Cook for 3-5min.
2. When the onions are translucent, add mushroom, garlic, smoked paprika, sweet paprika, onion powder, salt and pepper.
3. Cook mushrooms until they are soft.
4. Add tomato. Stir well, taste and adjust seasoning if needed.
5. Enjoy with rice and beans, and plantains on the side.

Egypt Koshari

INGREDIENTS
Layer 1: Wild Rice & Vermicelli
• 2/3 cup Wild Rice
• 4 tbsp Vermicelli
• 1 Onion, finely chopped
• 1 tbsp Olive oil
• 1 ½ cups Water, adjust if needed
Layer 2: Lentil
• 2/3 cup brown Lentil
• 1 Bay Leaf
• 3 cups Water
Layer 3: Pasta
• 2/3 cup Elbow Macaroni
• Water
• Salt, to taste
Layer 4: Chickpeas
• 1 ½ cups Chickpeas
Layer 5: Tomato sauce
• 1 cup Tomato Sauce
• 1 large Tomato, finely chopped
• 5 cloves Garlic, minced
• ½ tbsp Coriander powder
• ½ tbsp Cumin powder
• 1 tsp Chili flakes
• 1 tsp Vinegar
• ½ tsp Sugar
• Salt, to taste

Layer 6: Birista (fried onions)
• 1 large Onion, thinly sliced
• ½ tsp Cornflour
• Oil, for frying
Dressing
• 1 cup Water
• 2 tbsp White Vinegar
• 1 tsp Coriander powder
• 1 tsp Cumin powder
• 1 tsp Red Chili powder
• 1 tsp Red Chili flakes
• 3 cloves Garlic, minced
• Salt, to taste

INSTRUCTIONS

Layer 1 -Wild Rice & Vermicelli

1. Heat olive oil pot, sauté onion until starts to turn brown.
2. Add vermicelli and fry for 1-2 mins. Stir.
3. Add rice to pot and fry for 2-3 mins.
4. Add in salt and water. Cook until rice is done. Set aside.
    Layer 2: Lentil
5. Wash and soak lentil in warm water for 15-20 mins. if dry.
6. In a pot add lentil, water, bay leaf, and salt. Cook until lentils are tender but not too soft to where they are mushy.
7. Strain and set aside.
    Layer 3: Pasta
8. Add pasta to the boiling water and cook until tender. Set aside.
    Layer 4: Chickpeas
9. Warm chickpeas in a small pot. Set aside.
    Layer 5: Tomato sauce
10. In a saucepan, add all the ingredients listed for layer 5. Cook for approx.15 mins. Set aside.
    Layer 6: Birista (Fried onions)
11. In small bowl, mix onion and sprinkle corn flour
12. Heat oil in pan and deep fry the onions till golden brown.
13. Place onions on a paper towel covered plate and spread the onion to avoid sticking together.
14. To serve, spread a layer of rice & vermicelli first. Add lentil on top, then in order, add pasta, chickpeas, sauce, and fried onions. Pour dressing on top.

Mexico Mole Poblano & Enmoladas

INGREDIENTS

Mole Poblano Paste

- 7 Ancho Chiles
- 6 Mulato Chiles
- 6 Pasilla Chiles
- 3 Chipotle Chiles, dried
- 1 Onion, small
- 2-3 Roma Tomatoes
- 3 cloves Garlic
- 2/3 cup Raisins
- ¾ cup Raw Peanuts, unsalted
- 2/3 cup Almonds
- 1/3 cup Pumpkin seeds (pepitas)
- 1/3 cup Sesame seeds
- 2 Corn Tortillas, cut into fourths
- 1 bread roll sliced, make sure not made with milk
- 1 ripe Plantain, peeled & sliced
- 1 stick Ceylon Cinnamon, pieces
- 3 Cloves, cloves
- ½ tsp Anise seed
- ½ cone Piloncillo
- 1 tablet Ibarra Chocolate, or other vegan chocolate
- 1L Water OR Vegetable Stock
- 2 Bouillon Vegetable Cubes, optional
- 1 tsp Black Peppercorns
- Olive oil OR Avocado oil

Enmoladas

- Corn Tortillas
- 8 oz. Mushrooms, sliced
- ¼ Onion, thinly sliced

Garnish

- Toasted Sesame Seeds
- Crumbled Tofu
- Onions, sliced thinly
- Avocado

INSTRUCTIONS

Mole Poblano Paste

1. Remove seeds and stems from the dried chiles. In a cast iron pan, set medium heat to lightly toast the chiles.
2. Cover chiles with boiling water in a pot and soak for 20 mins.
3. Bring a medium pot of water to simmer and add garlic, tomato, and onion. Simmer for about 6-7 mins or until onion is tender. Strain and set aside.
4. Once the chiles are soft, place them in the blender with 1 cup of water. Blend until smooth. Strain and set aside.
5. On medium-high heat and add vegetable oil to large sauté pan.
6. Add raisins, pumpkin seeds, peanuts, almonds, tortilla, bread, and plantain one at a time until deep-golden brown.
7. Place all the fried ingredients in the blender. Add cinnamon, clove, anise seed, black peppercorns, and sesame seeds, 1 cup of water and blend. Add as much water as needed to blend mixture into a smooth thick sauce. Strain if needed and set aside.
8. On medium heat, add ½ cup of water, piloncillo, vegetable bouillon and chocolate to large pan. Stir until dissolves.
9. Add chile mixture and nut mixture to pan and mix thoroughly. Season to taste with salt and pepper.

10. Bring to low simmer and continue mixing constantly. Simmer for 15 mins. then remove from heat.

Enmoladas

1. Place 1 cup of mole poblano paste in medium sauce pot. Add ½ cup of water/ vegetable stock and bring to low simmer. Stir well; Add more water/ vegetable stock if needed.
2. Sauté onions and mushrooms until golden brown in a large pan. Season with salt and pepper to taste.
3. Soften your corn tortillas by heating them very briefly in the oven on 300`, be sure not to leave them in too long or they will get crunchy or burn.
4. Fill tortillas with mushroom mixture and roll. Serve on plate and pour mole poblano sauce on top.

Top with sesame seeds, onions, avocado and crumbled tofu.

Javon S. Wood

Hello world, my name is Javon Samuel Wood. I was born on June 9, 2007, in Staten Island University Hospital. I was named Javon because my mother wanted me to have my brother's middle name. I have 3 siblings, Tony, Quadia and Ray. In my culture it was claimed as bad luck if you had the same name as a sibling, but my mother didn't believe in that. My middle and last name came from my father, which makes his full name. I go by a few nicknames such as Toot, Jay and Von. One of my favorite earliest memories was going to Fun Station with my mother and my cousins. Some hobbies that I have are playing basketball, playing video games, and reading books. I am very proud of myself for how far I've come in life so far. Some days in life I've had thoughts that I wouldn't make it, but I continued to push through.

There are five facts about me that I would like to share. I am partially Jamaican and Honduran, I love reading, I write books, I play all different types of sports, and I'm vegan. What I like to do for fun is play video games. It calms me down when I'm mad or even just relaxes me. My favorite sport out of all is basketball. When I was around age 3 my father started to teach me about basketball. He put a mini hoop in my backyard for me to start practicing and as I got older, I started to use the bigger hoop that was there from when he was young, which my grandfather built for him. He taught me how to dribble and shoot. The first thing I remember was when he taught me how to shoot. Days and days went by, and I started to make more shots which inspired my favorite quote, "You miss 100% of the shots you don't take." In other words, you can't succeed unless you try.

Growing up in the area where I live, I've had many childhood struggles. For example, people shooting guns every day in the neighborhood, worrying about having food on the table, and having to watch my surroundings everywhere I go. I feel no person should go through that but luckily my family has always been there for me. I had both my mother's side of the family and my fathers. My family has had an impact on the way I act towards others and relationships. They taught me many life lessons on what I should do when encountering these things that I've experienced. Some of the most significant relationships in my life that have defined me the ones between my brother Tony D. Flash, my mother Catherine Simms, and my father Samuel Wood.

Between me and my brother his relationship is most important. He teaches me everything I need to know in life to be wealthy and successful. Without him I wouldn't be starting my own business. My father is like a mentor to me. Without him in my life I would be incomplete. He is like my other half. We do everything together. He taught me my favorite sport, basketball. My mother's relationship to me is very different. We talk about everything and love each other to the moon and back. All these relationships have defined me because the way the individuals speak to me changes how I think in life. One day I might be able to teach my kids the same thing they teach me.

I have some formal education, but I have mostly self-education. I learn about things by myself that a school wouldn't teach me. Now I am going to High School at St. Peters Boys High School. I haven't mastered any achievements yet but I'm almost there and continue to grow. My goal is to become an NBA player. Something I feel sets me apart from other people is how I interpret things around me such as where I live, the struggles I go through, etc. Matters of faith also have an impact on my life. I go to a private Catholic High School and my mother told me I'm Catholic. Special Situations do impact my life because those are the memories I want to remember. You are a buildup of all your memories.

The core knowledge I wish to impart is that freedom and wealth in this world is key, and all you need to remember, is that freedom and wealth is key. I believe if I keep working hard and keep a consistency, I will reach my goal in life. That should be for everyone in the world. Keep your head high. My name is Javon Samuel Wood and one day you will see me in the NBA.